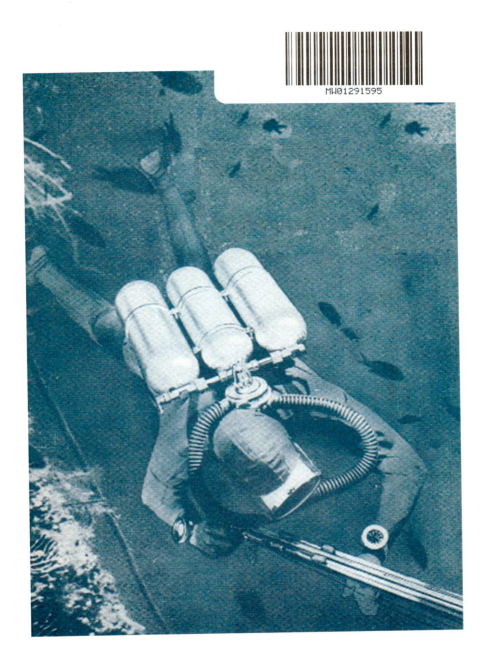

1

Table of contents

©2015 Brian Douglas

Primary Regulator and Alternate

The Aqua-Lung was invented in 1942 by Jacques Coustea and Emile Gagan. Since then it has gotten much better. In its original form, it is distinctly the iconic double hose regulator, for years they made improvements to its design. They breath easier, they mass produced it and it became utterly reliable. However, the double hose configuration was limited, and it is impossible for it to breath as well as a single hose regulator. The reason for this is the placement of the second stage and therefore, the performance of the regulator suffers. In a double hose regulator, the first and second stage is located clamped to the tank, so the pressure difference between your lungs and the aqualung is a significant variable that adds to the inefficiency of the double hose regulator, it was like breathing through a very long snorkel. Prior to the single hose regulator when the Coustea crew wanted to do some very deep diving the only way they could physically breathe at that depth was to manufacture high pressure hoses, which allowed them to carry the regulator mounted to their chest. The limitations of the double hose regulator became very clear and was eventually discontinued. With the advent of the single hose regulator, the second stage is directly in front of your mouth giving you the most accurate and correct pressure suitable for easy breathing. There have been so many improvements to the regulator from so many people and companies, which brings us to the modern regulator which is a joy to breathe from. Enjoy what more than 70 years of research and development has brought you. It has taken a long time to get to this point.

What is a primary regulator? A primary regulator consists of a first stage and one second stage.
What is an alternate? An alternate is your back-up second stage. There are numerous options available to suit your needs, including, octopus, spare air, pony bottle, integrated inflator and double tanks. Each of these choices contains advantages and disadvantages.

4

The octopus is an extra mouthpiece attached to your first stage
regulator. The advantages are, it is always there you can not forget
it in another bag or leave it on the boat by accident. This is most
likely the alternate you trained with during open water training and
having proper training with your gear is essential to your safety.
The disadvantages are, if your buddy runs out of air that means
you are also low on air, and now you have two divers draining a
low tank very quickly and there may not be enough air to make a
SAFE Ascent.

Spare Air is a small cylinder that holds about three cubic feet of air. It has its own built in regulator and is an independent air source. The advantages are, it is an independent air source it does not use the air from your scuba tank as a redundancy. If you run out of air, self rescue is very easy. If your buddy runs out of air, you can hand him the Spare Air and your buddy is not draining what is remaining of your air supply. The disadvantages are, it is a very small capacity air supply, and a direct ascent to the surface is required. It is not possible to both ascend and complete a safety stop on a Spare Air. This is not the best choice for any type of diving with an overhead environment such as wreck diving, or cavern diving.

A pony bottle is a little scuba tank with its own valve and any regulator you like can be used on this tank. The advantages of the pony bottle are, it is an independent air source, and it is larger than the Spare Air. Depending on the size you get a safety stop is possible. Sizes generally range from 6-30 cubic feet. The 13 cubic feet sized tanks seem to be the favorite it is a nice balance of size, weight and ease of carrying. The disadvantages are, you need another regulator, it will add weight, you can forget this at home or on the boat, and it will take a bit longer to set up your equipment before the dive.

An integrated alternate inflator, is an alternate air source, which is combined to function as your low pressure inflator and alternate air source. It is attached to a specialized quick disconnect fitting. It is still a low pressure hose, however, the flow rate is increased to give enough air to breath. A standard low pressure inflator hose will not give you a high enough flow rate to breathe off of. The advantages are, compactness, if you travel you can eliminate a hose, less dangles and it is always at the ready you can't forget this as it is now part of your BCD. The disadvantages are, once again if your buddy runs out of air two divers are draining a low tank. Additionally, this alternate inflator has additional procedures that complicate an out of air emergency. The problem with the alternate inflator is the procedure for donating air to a buddy is to give your primary regulator to your buddy, and then the donor switches to the alternate inflator. Temporarily, both divers will be out of air during the transition, and it will be more difficult to vent the expanding air from your BCD on ascent.

If you decide to wear double tanks, it is a mixed blessing. An entire redundant system is available for you to utilize, however, weigh the benefits of limited mobility VS portability, tanks are heavy.

Pre-Dive regulator Checklist

Just as a pilot will do a preflight checklist, you owe it to yourself and your buddy to perform a pre-dive checklist on your regulator. The regulator is a critical piece of equipment, which must be in good working order. It's an even better idea to do this a week or month before you plan to dive.

1: Service date.
When was it last serviced? Depending on the usage it gets ranging from rental gear to your own personal equipment, it should be serviced every three months to a year. Rental equipment gets a lot of use. Personal equipment is capable of surviving much longer service intervals because it is used less frequently, and you are capable of providing the proper rinsing it should receive. Personal equipment should be serviced every 12 months when properly cared for.

2: Inspect hoses.
Look at the hoses, search the entire length for defects. Defects will appear as dry rot, cracks, splits, cuts and bubbles. Once this is done pull the hose protectors away from the first stage and inspect the hoses under the protectors. Inspect this area in four positions yoke screw down, yoke screw up, then hoses going with gravity and hoses going against gravity, reinstall the hose protectors.

3&4: Test Torque
Sometimes a hose will appear to be in perfect working order. However, it has only been installed hand tight, or it has worked itself loose. Grasp the hose end near the first stage and try to turn the hose counterclockwise, it should not budge. Then move down

the hose and do the same to the nut connected to the second stage and repeat this process on all hoses and second stages. If they are loose, it will spin freely using nothing more than your hands. If they spin, the fitting needs to be tightened snug. All that is required is a wrench and a light touch, do not put elbow grease into tightening these fittings, they work using o-ring seals not force. Always snug never tight, if you can't remove it using your hands, it's good enough.

5: Inspect cable ties.

Look at your mouthpiece, they should have a clamp or a cable tie on them. If it is a clamp, make sure it is secured all around and not cracked. If it is a cable tie, first off, make sure it is not missing. Next take a look at the end of the cable tie, if they are cut wrong they can be razor sharp and slice through the skin as easily as a razor..

6: Tug on the mouthpiece.

Tug on the mouthpiece, it should not pull off. If it does pull off, it can mean a few things. Either the cable tie was not tight or the mouthpiece is the wrong size. There are not many size mouthpieces but there are a few, and if you put a big mouthpiece on a regulator built for a small mouthpiece, it will slip right off no matter how tight you zip that cable tie.

7: Inspect mouthpiece for holes.

The two areas where this is most common are the bite tabs and the circumference. Inspect the bite tabs from both directions top and bottom. To inspect the circumference tug on the mouthpiece inspecting it all around looking for a small hole. If you feel a trickle of water during the dive, this may be the cause. A better way to inspect for holes in the mouthpiece is to remove it with a pair of wire cutters and stretch the material, pull the bite tabs and the back of the mouthpiece apart looking for light.

8: Inspect for major defects.

Look for big obvious signs, a hole in the second stage cover, corrosion or cracks. If it doesn't look good, odds are it will not perform well either. When a crack forms, the only fact is the crack will get bigger. Whatever is cracked must be replaced.

9: Inspect the filter.
Unscrew the yoke screw then remove the dust cap and on most regulators, you should be able to see the filter. It is a mesh wire screen in the shape of a cone or a flat circular screen. It comes in a few colors, copper, silver, brown, and I'm sure a few other colors I haven't seen. The one color a filter should never be is green. If a filter is green that means water has gotten inside the regulator, and it needs service.

10: Air test.
Smell the air, first smell the air in the tank without hooking up the regulator. If the air smells like anything other than air, for example diesel, it is a bad fill. Don't use it. Next hook up the regulator, turn the air on and purge the regulator. Take a big smell of that air but don't breathe it. I have had quite a few memorable regulators that I have had come in for service. One particular has become a sort of a legend, every time the story is told it gets more horrible, and it has grown to the point where the upstairs office started to get choked up from the stench which was emitted from this regulator. The reality of the situation was as follows. Somehow an excessive amount of water got into this regulator, and it sat there for a long time. In the time the water was sitting in the regulator it acted like a Petrie dish growing bacteria and fungus. When it finally came in for service, I hooked it up and a smell came out of that regulator that I can only describe as the biggest smelliest rotten pile of garbage imaginable. The first stage was infected, the second stages were infected, and all hoses were infected. Luckily, I only had to evacuate the regulator repair room for about five minutes while it aired out. If the air doesn't smell like air, don't use the regulator. Not only is it dangerous, it can be bad for your

respiratory system. You might even get an infection. Take care of your regulator and this will never happen to you.

11: Purge test.
Push the purge button and then release. If the air flow stops, it's good. If you have to put your thumb over the mouthpiece to stop the flow of air, it's also good, that is called a free flow, which I will cover in detail shortly. What is not acceptable is if after you stop the flow of air you hear a leak. If there is a leak, the regulator needs service.

12: Pressure Gauge.
When you purge the regulator, the pressure gauge needle should move smoothly. It should not be jumpy, and it should zero out when you can no longer purge. If it is jumpy, more than likely there is some corrosion caused by water going on in the pressure gauge, and it should be serviced or replaced.

13: Test fittings.
Sometimes your BCD will not allow the quick disconnect fitting to connect or vice versa. This is caused by marine growth, water deposits or a lose Schrader valve.
Inside the coupling of your quick disconnect fitting, if you look closely, you will see your Schrader valve. That valve is removable and, if it has worked its way loose, it needs to be retightened, a pair of fine tweezers may work, if not try the auto parts store, look for a Schrader valve tool, and of course, your local dive center will have no trouble tightening your Schrader valve for you.

14: Suction test.
To perform this test have the dust cap on the regulator or the regulator on the tank and the valve closed. Simply put the regulator in your mouth like you were diving and try to inhale. If you can get any sort of satisfying breath out of the regulator, it can

mean you have a leak, which can be several things such as, a hole in the diaphragm, a bad seat, leaky exhaust valve, a hole in the mouthpiece or numerous other things. However, this test can be misleading to the consumer, when a repair technician performs this test, no mouthpiece is installed and the connection to the hose end is plugged minimizing the possibilities to misdiagnose the problem. Regardless, if you can get a good breath off your regulator when the air isn't on, you have a problem, and it should be serviced.

15: Subjective Breathing
Your pre-dive checklist is now complete. If it passed all the preceding tests go ahead and see how it breathes.

Mouthpieces removal and Replacement

The most abundant problem with regulators is the mouthpieces. To change a mouthpiece you have two options. The cable tie or the clamp, the cable tie can be removed with a pair of wire cutters. After installing a new mouthpiece put the cable tie into the mouthpiece groove and pull it tight using a pair of needle nose pliers. At this point you have a few options for about 20 dollars you can buy a nice cable tie gun that will trim it perfectly. You can leave the tail on the cable tie, it won't harm anybody but it will be a bit annoying. You can cut the tail off with a pair of wire cutters and chance slicing yourself with a sharp edge that remains on there, if you don't cut it just perfect. Lastly, you can cut it with a pair of wire cutters and spend a few minutes filling the edges of the cable tie down until they are perfectly smooth and can't cut anything. I recommend getting a mouthpiece clamp, if you bite through more than your share of mouthpieces. Just carry along a little screwdriver so you can work the lever on the clamp, and life will get a lot easier.

Free flows, what and why

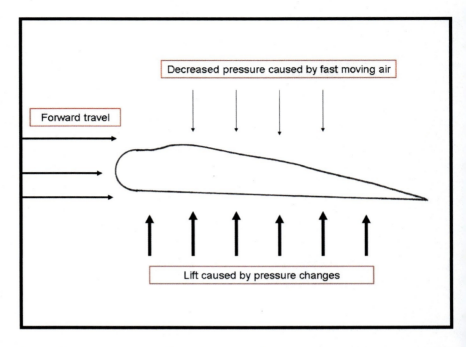

How does an airplane fly? It moves forward and accelerates at that point air hits the wing and has two choices, go above the wing or go below the wing. The air above the wing moves faster than the air below the wing. Fast moving air creates less pressure allowing the air pressure to push up on the wing creating lift resulting in flight. This same force is responsible for causing your regulator to free flow. A free flow is typically not a malfunction.

Think of a regulator, hit the purge button. That purge creates fast moving air causing a decrease in pressure, that decrease in pressure allows the ambient pressure to push on the diaphragm of your second stage resulting in a free flow that will not stop unless the balance of pressure is restored. The solution to a free flowing regulator is **not** to bash it on a rock as hard as you can. The solution is to restore the balance of pressure that can be done by slowing down the air exiting the mouthpiece by either turning the regulator over or placing your thumb over the mouthpiece.

A true regulator malfunction free flow will typically be caused by one of two things, a high pressure seat failure or cold water freeze up. A high pressure seat failure can be detected by both second stages free flowing at the same time. If only one second stage free flows, it is probably not a high pressure seat failure. A cold water free flow can be caused by a few things.

A cold water freeze up can be either a first stage or a second stage problem. The first stage can freeze up on a cold water dive in a manner which will mimic a high pressure seat failure. On a regulator not specifically built for cold water there exists a space where water will collect and this space is where the intermediate pressure of the first stage is set. What happens is water freezes in this space, expands and throws off the pressure. This will cause both second stages to free flow. Another place ice can build up is on the crown seat area. When you inhale air pressure in this area drops from 3,000 psi to approximately 150 psi, mathematically the temperature drops to -55 degrees below zero F. That's pretty darn cold. When Ice forms on this area it is incapable of making a proper seal and starts a free flow cycle, which will cause a bad free flow very quickly.
 However, bring the regulator into a warm location let it thaw out and the problem will resolve itself unlike a true high pressure seat failure, which can only be fixed by having the regulator serviced. A second stage cold water freeze up will also be caused by ice buildup, however, in this case only the second stage will free flow. What happens in the second stage is ice forms and builds up on the sealing surfaces between the seat preventing the demand valve from closing after you take a breath. Another location ice may build up is on the demand lever itself. This build up of ice will build between the diaphragm and the lever pushing the demand lever down and increasing the flow of air, which only creates more ice build up until an out of control free flow is present.

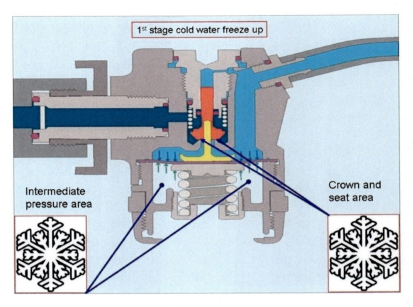

1st stage cold water freeze up

Intermediate pressure area

Crown and seat area

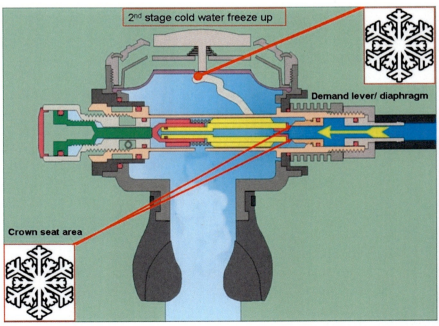

2nd stage cold water freeze up

Demand lever/ diaphragm

Crown seat area

There are a few steps you can take to minimize the chance of a cold water free flow. Regulators have a temperature rating, if you plan on diving in cold water, which is typically defined as below 60-55 degrees F don't buy a warm water regulator.

Some regulators have an "environmental seal." What an environmental seal does is it protects the first stage. It is basically a gasket that adds another layer of protection to the regulator. For example during your surface interval water can collect in the spring area where pressures are set freeze, expand and cause a free flow. An environmental seal will not allow this to happen.

Then during your dive the environmental seal acts as an insulator. Imagine the diaphragm of your regulator is made out of play dough. When it is warm it is very soft and pliable. It operates normally and has no problems flexing and bending. When it gets cold we all know you can't have fun with play dough, it becomes hard, brittle and a bear to work with. This stiffness is what causes a free flow, the regulator diaphragm will freeze in the open position and will not allow the regulator to close. Keep imagining the diaphragm of your regulator is made of play dough, to preserve the pliability of the diaphragm. It must be insulated from the water by an environmental seal. By doing this the diaphragm stays much warmer, pliable and performs much better under cold water conditions.

If you plan on a lot of cold water diving, maybe a season of ice diving, it is possible for the regulator tech to detune your regulator so it can handle a bit more ice build up than normal. It won't breathe as well, but it will be less likely to free flow.
Don't breathe off your regulator until it's underwater. Air is a great insulator, it will preserve ice and make it easier for your regulator to free flow. Water is a great conductor of heat it will thaw the ice trying to form up to a certain point. Basically, if you

breathe off your regulator before it is submerged, you are pre-icing the surfaces, and, if you don't breathe off it until it is underwater, you are defrosting the surfaces.

Lastly pack your bag the night before but don't leave the regulator stuck in a cold car. The night before bring it into a nice warm house, it needs all the help it can get to avoid free flowing the next day.

Care and Maintence

The easiest way to properly care for our regulator is to rinse it properly after every day of diving. Depending on your situation, there are several ways you can accomplish this. The best way is to use a dunk tank of fresh water, which is constantly getting flushed out. The next best way is to use a hose of steady flowing water. The worst way, which can force water into places it shouldn't be and damage delicate rubber parts, would be to take a high pressure water nozzle to your gear, this should be avoided at all costs.

Several scenarios you may encounter involving rinsing your equipment include, perfect conditions, ideal conditions, delayed conditions and compromised conditions.

In the perfect world, it would always be easy to take care of your gear. You would get out of the water and there would be a huge bucket of fresh water that gets flushed out every few minutes waiting for you. Under perfect conditions, hook the regulator up to the tank turn on the air and lower the tank valve and regulator first stage into the water along with the hoses second stages pressure gauge and quick disconnect hose. Then jiggle the tank around to work out any air pockets hiding in the first stage, shake the second stages and purge them too. When you purge the second stages, you get fresh water in those hard to reach spots, and if you have a piston first stage purging your second stages will assist in removing deposits from the first stage if it is submerged in fresh water. Finally pull your tank and regulator out of the water, purge the second stages until they are dry also shaking water out at the same time, turn off the air, purge the system, remove from the tank, dry and install the dust cap. In the perfect world you would perform this rinse right after a day of diving.

Under ideal conditions, you are still capable of properly rinsing your regulator, and it will be rinsed after a day of diving. Hook your regulator up to a tank and turn it on. Using a hose with a nice steady flow run water over the first stage hoses and pressure gauge. To properly rinse the second stages run water on the outside additionally it is vital to rinse the internal parts of the second stages. Take the hose and direct the flow of water into the mouthpiece, you should see water flowing out of the regulators exhaust valve, let it flow for about five seconds then purge it a few times. Purge the second stages until they are dry, also shaking water out at the same time, turn off the air, purge the system, remove from the tank and install your dry dust cap.

Delayed conditions, would be on a dive boat, you dive all day get home later, and you don't have a tank of air to perform a rinse. In this case, many of the same rules apply. Keep in mind that because you do not have a tank of air purging the regulator during the rinse can cause harm to it. Make sure the dust cap is secure, using a hose that has a good steady flow rinse the first stage and hoses. Rinse the outside of the second stage and as always take the hose and direct the flow of water into the mouthpiece, you should see water flowing out of the regulators exhaust valve, let it flow for about five seconds **do not** push the purge button. Shake the water out and let it drip dry.

Compromised conditions, would be conditions such as a multi-day live-aboard or a deserted island where fresh water is scarce and for several days proper care of your regulator is difficult or impossible. In these situations, your best bet may be to take a glass of fresh water pour it into the mouthpiece then clear it. Once the vacation has ended, and you get into more ideal conditions hook it up to a tank and let is soak in a dunk tank for awhile.

With the volatile nature of salt water being what it is my favorite way to end a vacation is to plan my last dive in a fresh water spring. The water there is cleaner than most of the well water across the country and making the last dive of my vacation there does a better job of rinsing my gear than I could at home. If you have the opportunity I highly recommend considering adding a fresh water spring such as those found in Florida to your dive plan. Lastly, to keep sand and gravel out of your regulator it's a great idea to protect it with a padded regulator bag.

Purchase Considerations

When you are ready to buy a regulator Warranty and factory support play a huge role in determining the quality of a regulator. Aqua-Lung is a great company. When I call them up the technical support staff is excellent. If I have a problem with a regulator, odds are they have had hundreds of technicians prior to me call in with the exact same problem, and they can give me a factory certified solution to my problem. I have also had the unfortunate fate to call in with a problem they have never heard of before, and they spent enormous amounts of time on the phone with me eventually we solved the problem. The warranty for every company is a bit different, generally, if you bring it in for service every year, parts are free and the only charge is for labor. Be sure to confirm the warranty policy of any company before you invest in a regulator, buyer beware.

Service Over Simplified

The basic steps to servicing a regulator are, an evaluation, disassembly, cleaning, rebuild/lubricate, tune the performance and file the warranty with the factory.

The evaluation is performed at the start, so I know what kind of problems pre-exist if any. I perform the pre-dive check plus a check on the intermediate pressure, spending one minute to evaluate a regulator will tell me most of the information I need to know and what to expect when I open it up.

During disassembly, I can learn quite a few things about the diver and about the previous technician who worked on the regulator. I have opened alternates, which looked like sandboxes, I have been forced to use breaker bars and clamps to open body's which should have been hand tight but were corroded solid and boiling a brass body to convince a part to budge. All of which are signs of diver neglect. At the same time, I do learn a bit about the previous technician. Did they use the correct lubricant, how tight are the inner fittings fastened, is it missing o-rings, are there extra O-rings, are they factory o-rings or are they from the hardware store? All of this tells me whether or not they are factory trained and certified to work on this regulator or are they making things up as they go along. This is why having a factory trained technician is so important. Parts can go in backwards, it isn't enough to simply put it back together the way you found it. It must operate to factory specifications and have all the o-rings in all the right spots no more no less.

All metal parts are cleaned using a hydro-sonic cleaner and solution. This machine acts like a million tiny little pressure washers removing all deposits and corrosion. Plastic and rubber parts are cleaned using the approved methods then it is rinsed in fresh water and dried. Hose fittings, including the quick disconnect fitting are also cleaned at this time.

At this time, the use of factory parts kits are utilized. All o-rings have been removed prior to cleaning. Now the new o-rings are properly lubricated and installed. The use of factory o-rings is vital to the performance of your regulator. Companies spend weeks, months, years and decades of research and development into what appears as a simple o-ring. However, they have built it to operate effectively in every thermal region of the world from Siberia to the Caribbean. The o-ring is the best composition, the best size, the best hardness. It is the best! And, if any other o-ring is used you are gambling with your life. Make sure your service center uses factory kits to rebuild your regulator, accept no substitutions. A good sign of factory parts is packaging. Many factory kits come with an index card sized insert with the company name and regulator model printed on it. Others come with very bold labels of the company and regulator model. However, if you see a bag that looks generic that looks like it came from a hardware store, that is a good indication that you are getting cheap parts, and corners are getting cut.

Tune and paperwork, just like instruments in a band. If a regulator is not properly tuned, it will provide a horrible performance. Final pressures are set, and breathing effort is optimized. Finally, records are sent to the factory, and you also will receive a record to indicate what service was performed on the regulator as well as what parts were replaced.

Most regulators are serviced without any problems. However, it is a good practice to bring your regulator in one month before you need it. The reason being it may have a defective part inside and in all odds, the part is covered under warranty. However, if you need your regulator tomorrow overnight shipping is expensive and could end up costing you more than the complete regulator service.

Parts and Operation

The operation of any regulator is very simple, there are a couple of critical parts which once you understand the regulator becomes much less alien to you. There are also many parts that assist in the operation of a regulator. However, for the purposes of understanding how a regulator works, understanding the assisting parts is not vital and I will be over simplifying the regulator. There are many aspects to its operation, which a book can not explain.

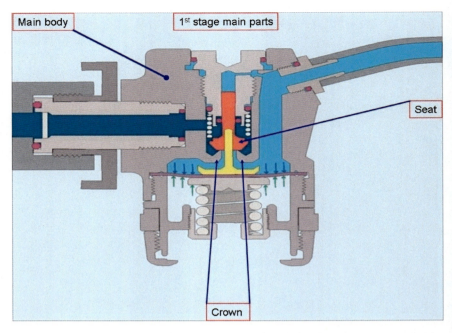

1st stage main parts

Main body

Seat

Crown

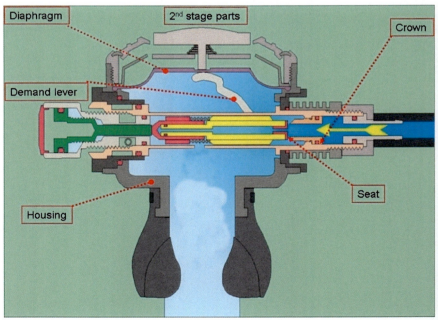

Diaphragm

2nd stage parts

Crown

Demand lever

Seat

Housing

The primary parts of a regulator first stage are the main body, seat and crown. The main body houses all the components and protects them from the elements. The seat, this is a dynamic part meaning it moves freely inside the regulator body, is made of a hard nylon material that can withstand the forces of 4,000 psi of air pressure yet still be pliable enough to form a nice seal at 200 psi like a rubber gasket would. The crown is basically a nozzle. The primary parts of your second second stage are the crown, seat, housing, diaphragm and demand lever, think of the demand lever as the pistol grip lever on your garden hose.

Think of your regulator as a house water system. The house is connected to the city's water supply, think of the city's water supply as your scuba tank. The scuba tank fills your water heater, think of your water heater as the first stage, the first stage holds a good amount of air and is constantly ready to deliver it to a second stage when it has a demand for it. What acts as the second stage is your garden hose. Inhale and suction pulls on a diaphragm this diaphragm acts on the demand lever just as your hand will activate a garden nozzle when it pushes on it, the garden nozzle is the demand lever, when you push on it, it delivers air when you stop it is sealed and stops the flow., This is exactly how a demand lever in a second stage works. When it comes down to the basics, a regulator can not get any simpler.

The regulator is more than likely the most expensive collection of equipment and has the most that can go wrong with it. Unfortunately, most of my horror stories are about regulators. There have been many misfortunes, which have been inflicted upon an innocent regulator. Not rinsing a regulator will cause deposits to build up on the crown causing a nasty leak. Installing a wet dust cap, leaving the dust cap off will introduce water into the first stage and hoses causing growth in the regulator creating a massive stink bomb. Sand will scratch soft plastic parts causing bad leaks. Excessive heat will melt rubber diaphragms in your second stage destroying them. Corrosion will weld parts together. And heavy impacts can crack a plastic body creating more leaks. Treat your regulators well if you take care of it, it will take care of you.

How do you know if the stream of water your using to rinse your regulator is just right or too strong?   Ask yourself, if I had to wash something out of my eye would I use this stream of water. If the answer is yes go ahead and rinse your regulator, if not readjust.

"AQUA-LUNG" REGULATORS

Cousteau-Gagnan Patent No. 2485039

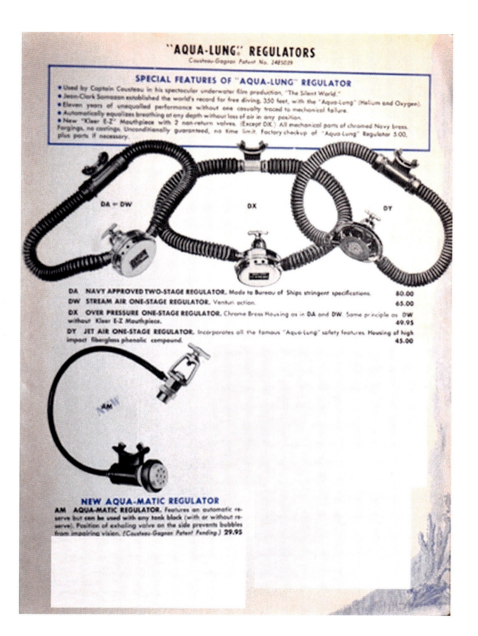

DA   NAVY APPROVED TWO-STAGE REGULATOR. Made to Bureau of Ships stringent specifications.   80.00

DW   STREAM AIR ONE-STAGE REGULATOR. Venturi action.   65.00

DX   OVER PRESSURE ONE-STAGE REGULATOR. Chrome Brass Housing as in DA and DW. Same principle as DW without Kleer E-Z Mouthpiece.   49.95

DY   JET AIR ONE-STAGE REGULATOR. Incorporates all the famous "Aqua-Lung" safety features. Housing of high impact fiberglass phenolic compound.   45.00

NEW AQUA-MATIC REGULATOR

AM   AQUA-MATIC REGULATOR. Features an automatic reserve but can be used with any tank block (with or without reserve). Position of exhaling valve on the side prevents bubbles from impairing vision. (Cousteau-Gagnan Patent Pending.) **29.95**

SPG and Depth Gauge

The Submersible pressure gauge, I cannot phantom the thought of going diving without a pressure gauge. The thought of not knowing how much air I have remaining is terrifying. The submersible pressure gauge did not start to gain popularity until the late 1960's. Further investigation led me in the direction of archived US Divers catalogs from the early years. The earliest catalog that had a submersible pressure gauge was 1957. In 1957, the double hose regulator was still the flagship regulator, US Divers had four regulators for sale in 1957 three of those regulators were double hose regulators, only one single hose regulator was up for sale, and this was before a regulator was filled with ports for accessory hoses.

How did the pressure gauge of 1957 work? They work exactly as the pressure gauges of today work. Inside your pressure gauge, you will find a metal coil. When the gauge is pressurized air tries to straighten out this coil bending it and through a series of calibrated gears, your cylinder pressure is determined and displayed to you in an easy to read dial. The function of the analog pressure gauge has not changed much at all over the years, however, they have gotten more user friendly.

UNDERWATER PRESSURE GAUGES

These pressure gauges indicate air content of tank while diving, or at any other time. Permits dives to be planned safely while submerged. Can be used only with "J" valve on single tank block and any of our two tank manifold valves by proper drilling at one end of the manifold. Installation instructions packed with each gauge.

1766 PRESSURE GAUGE WITH DIAL. Flexible Shaft and Stainless Steel Water Tight Case.   **19.95**

1755 STATIONARY GAUGE.   **8.95**

In 1957, regulators were not equipped with ports for accessories that are now mandatory such as the low pressure inflator hose, alternate air source, and submersible pressure gauge. The regulator was nothing more than a primary air source so it was a trick to use a pressure gauge. The solution of the day was to attach a hose to the tank valve, at the end of the hose was the pressure gauge which could be read by the diver underwater. This was possible for the day because the valve handle was located on the top of the valve, the reserve "J" valve was on the left, and this allowed the right side of the valve to be adapted for a pressure gauge, on a few select models of valves. I cannot speak with first hand knowledge of why the submersible pressure gauge did not catch on, but I have a few good reasons why I believe it took so long. Once the pressure gauge was installed in a valve it could not be removed easily, the cylinder would have to be drained to remove it. Once you have this pressure gauge on there it is always there swinging around, prone to damage, and it makes it more difficult to pack tanks for travel, the reserve "J" valve was a lot easier to pack. Price, in 1957 you could buy a top of the line double hose regulator for $80.00, the cost of this pressure gauge, which would have been dedicated to a cylinder because it's non-removable was $20.00. The early SPG was a labor-intensive and an expensive product that did not catch on, it wasn't until the late 1960's that it became a popular product.

In the late 1960's the single hose regulator started to surpass the popularity of the double hose with superior performance. Part of its performance was the ease at which it could be machined to accept accessories such as the SPG. In the 1966 US Divers catalog, there is an SPG which can be installed easily on any current model single hose regulator, and the cost was only $22.95. It can be moved from one tank to the next with your regulator, simplifying operation and reducing cost. This is very similar to the SPG that you know today.

Keep in mind that the SPG is a mechanical device, and it has tolerances. Its accuracy may not be true as you think it is, which is why it is always a good idea to plan to end a dive with an ample reserve of air remaining. This is a delicate instrument. It is a metal coil attached to a series of calibrated gears. Make sure to clip it off to yourself, it does not like to be dragged through the mud and get whacked on rocks.

The Depth gauge is similar in a few ways it also has tolerances, and you may be deeper than you are being told. Plan your dive conservatively so you have a fudge factor to fall back on. It also operates using a metal coil and a series of calibrated gears. It also has differences.

The type of pressure it senses is not tank pressure through a flexible hose. The pressure it senses is water pressure, and it must be built differently to sense this pressure. An SPG is sealed tight. A Depth gauge is filled with clear, vacuum packed oil. It is built with oil because it requires a non-compressible median to transmit the pressure to the inner metal coils and gears, this style of depth gauge is called a "Bourdon tube." If it did not use oil it would require a hole to transmit the pressure, and this hole would get clogged with mud, sand, and salt crystals, rendering your depth gauge useless and prone to failure after short periods of use, these gauges do exist and they are called "Capillary" depth gauges. Lastly, the oil is vacuum packed, why? Look at a container of cooking oil you will notice plenty of air bubbles in it. These air bubbles are not good for calibration and make reading the dial difficult. Vacuum packing the oil removes these air bubbles increasing the accuracy and readability. Every now and then, you will see a less than perfect depth gauge with a little bubble in it. That is an air bubble from improperly vacuumed oil or a bad seal on the depth gauge, which allows air into the gauge.

The oil filled depth gauge is only accurate up to an altitude of 1,000 feet above sea level. Above this altitude, additional procedures and or equipment is required. The easiest way to learn this is to take an altitude diver specialty course. In the course, you will learn theoretical vs actual depth, safety factors that you should take into consideration. Additional limitations altitude places upon you, and how to account for diving at one altitude and traveling to another altitude.

When a good regulator goes bad.

The good

It was a very pleasant April day. Most divers were getting ready for the season which meant I had a good deal of work cut out for me. My wall of regulators which consists of a square metal grid made out of wire with many hooks protruding from it was overflowing with regulators. It was a jumbled mess of hoses and to remove a single regulator I had to treat the wall like a balanced deck of cards.

From the wall of regulators I picked up An Aqualung Titan-LX Supreme, an extremely well priced high value regulator, which almost any diver would be satisfied. This is a middle of the line regulator. It is not cheap and at the same time it is not a luxury regulator. It is a work horse regulator, and it was my job to rebuild this regulator.

I took a few steps over to my computer and input the serial number, the serial number on most regulators is stamped or laser etched onto a highly visible part of the first stage and is also marked on the second stage. The first stage and second stage typically share the same serial number, however, the alternate has a different serial number. The computer completed its search and this regulator is due for a rebuild.

Before beginning to take anything apart a complete function check is performed. Beginning with a visual inspection of all hoses, the length is inspected for cracking, splitting, cuts, abrasion, bubbles and anything out of the ordinary. Each hose is inspected through its length and 360" hoses like to hide problems in natural bends. The hoses turned out to be in perfect shape.

The next step is ensuring the regulator is securely fastened. I grasp the hose ends at the first stage and give them a good twist counter clockwise, they do not budge then I turn my attention to the hose ends near the second stages and find as well they are securely fastened. With that behind me I turn my attention to the mouthpieces, ensuring they are secured properly I give them a tug and they are held solid. Then I remove the mouthpiece and give it a meticulous inspection looking for bites, tears and holes. Then I pull and stretch the mouthpiece in many directions in an attempt to show any signs of damage. The last thing anybody wants is to constantly be inhaling and choking on water, which is exactly what a small hole in the mouthpiece will cause.

At this point I take a big step back and take a general look at everything that could be wrong, cracked covers, body's missing caps, has somebody tried to fix something with silicon caulking, epoxy, superglue or the good old fashioned duct tape?   Thankfully this regulator is in perfect shape.

Normally at this point I'd take a look at the filter looking for green spots and signs of salt. If I see any signs of that I know it will be a very "fun" regulator to work on,   but this regulators filter is internal aside from that everything else is in great shape.

After all of this I finally get to hook it up to the test bench, which has so many buttons, switches, meters and gauges, that it does not take much of an imagination to turn it into a cockpit of a jetliner. In essence, it is a stainless steel and wooden box with about four valves. One valve is a regular scuba tank valve that I use to attach regulators to the test bench. Another valve turns it on and off. The third valve is a pressure regulator which is used to simulate pressure changes as a diver drains the tanks. With this pressure regulator I can have 4,500 psi, but I can limit the pressure to my work to whatever I want from 3,000 psi, 1,000 psi, 500 psi and everything in between.   This allows me to test the regulator on a full and an empty tank without heavy lifting. The fourth valve is a redundant purge button to purge the system before I remove the regulator form the test bench. There are two very large dial gauges. One displays Intermediate pressure and the other measures breathing effort. Two standard size gauges that tell me tank pressure and another gauge connected to the pressure control valve.

I screw the regulator onto the valve. I attach the quick disconnect coupling of the BC hose to a brass fitting and turn on the air. Air comes rushing out of the hose, it is clean dry air, so now I plug everything together for a proper test. The intermediate pressure (which is the air pressure delivered to the second stage) is in the proper range and is stable. I now have a complete assessment of this regulator and its condition and I am ready to tear it down.

With my wrench I loosen the hoses connecting to the first stage with ease, then I reach down and loosen the hose connections at the second stage. I set my wrench to the side. Getting back to business, I remove the second stages from the hoses and put those to the side. Then I remove all port plugs and hoses from the first stage and set the first stage down. I remove the o-rings from the port plugs, the second stage hoses have two o-rings that get removed, the male end is an external o-ring and the female end is a captive o-ring the requires a little patience to remove. The BCD hose has both Schrader valve and o-ring removed. The High pressure hose, spg may also be disassembled cleaned and rebuilt at this time rebuilding it consists of two small o-rings on a swivel connection Once all the hoses have their o-rings removed they are placed in the sonic cleaner where corrosion is removed.

While the sonic cleaner is working on the hoses, I turn my attention back to the first stage regulator. Servicing the first stage starts off by threading a tool into the high pressure port. The HP port is used because it is larger than the LP port as such more force can be exerted on it and less stress to the threads will be caused.

$$P = \frac{F}{A}$$

Once the tool is installed into the HP port the tool is clamped into a vise and the real work can begin. Using a selection or wrenches I remove the yoke and associated o-rings. On the top end I remove the environmental seal and piston, adjusting screw spring and pad, diaphragm and I carefully tip the regulator over to remove the pin. On the bottom end I remove the plug balancing chamber, spring seat and always last but not least the crown. All the o-rings are removed and the metal parts go into a pile and I turn my attention to the second stage.

Again I grab the spanner wrench and loosen the covers and remove the diaphragm, similar to checking the mouthpieces for holes I inspect the diaphragm for holes as well. I loosen the retaining nut on the right side of the regulator which allows me to remove the heat sink and then pop the entire second stage assembly out of the body. On the left side a retaining pin holds in the finely tuned adjustments, seat spring and balance chamber. On the right side is the coarse adjustment, mainly the crown. These fittings simply unscrew with an Allen head key and a flat blade screwdriver. Once more I remove all o-rings put the metal parts into a pile with my first stage parts and continue on.

Now that some time has passed my hoses are now cleaned. They are rinsed in fresh water, dried with an air gun and the o-rings replaced, as well as the swivel in the submersible pressure gauge.

Finally, I have room in the sonic cleaner for regulator parts, so in they go. While I am waiting for the parts to clean it is a great time to switch out the old o-rings, seats and such for new ones. Until you do a few hundred regulators you will be using the old o-rings as your guide, as to which size o-rings go where. Even when you are fluent with a regulator it is a good idea to use the old o-rings as a guide.

Once the regulator parts are cleaned rinsed and dried, it's time to put everything back together. O-rings are lubricated with an oxygen safe lubricant called cristolube and the o-rings are installed. Cristolube has no known freezing point as it is also used as a lubricant by NASA. To simplify things, a regulator goes back together the opposite way it came apart. Caution is required not to over torque parts, as more torque is never a good thing.

Once assembled the regulator is ready to be tuned. The first stage only has one adjustment made with an Allen wrench. That adjustment is called the intermediate pressure which is critical for your second stage to function properly.

The second stage has coarse and fine adjustments. The second stage tuning is basically a balancing act. On the right side I have the coarse adjustment, which I control with a "pneumatically balanced in-line adjustable screw driver." On the left I have a counterbalance pressure adjustment, which I control with a small Allen key. In a nutshell the coarse adjustment allows the regulator to seal and the fine adjustment allows the regulator to breath like a dream.

After all this work I finally get to update the file on the regulator, perform a second check on it, followed by a submersion check and I am done. This is Regulator service 101 with a good regulator in good shape with everything going the right way. It is very different when a good regulator goes bad.

The Bad

When a good regulator goes bad, they go bad in a big way and it is not always visibly apparent until a closer look is taken. It does not matter how little or how much money you spend on a regulator, they all must be taken care of equally well. A $1500 regulator will go just as bad as a $400 regulator. The following is one of the worst horror stories I have had the displeasure of working on through the years.

I'm getting ready to rebuild a regulator. During the function check I've hooked up the BCD coupler to a brass fitting and turn on the valve. Out shoots a stream of foul polluted nasty stinking water, which stinks up the entire repair room and it's basically evacuated for the next 10 minutes. This was a $1500 titanium regulator, which the owner thought was impervious to anything he could throw at it, and he was mistaken. The end result was the hoses got tossed in the trash, however, his primary hose was a hundred dollar hose with an integrated ball swivel so I had to find a way to salvage the hose, this turned out to be a two day long soak in Simple Green, after one day of soaking I changed the water because all the growth that came out of the hose turned the water black. Finally I cleaned the regulator and returned it to him.

Regulators are built with straight non tapered threads, which means an o-ring seal with minimal torque force is sufficient for sealing force. However, there is always somebody out there who doesn't care and says that's nothing but a load of bologna. So, here are a few things every diver should know that will help you sniff out bologna and find competent team members to dive with and fix your equipment.

The "core fundamentals" of regulator operation maintaince and service has remained largely unchanged for more than 40 years. It is very easy to locate a leak with a spray bottle of soapy water, just spray it all over and look for the bubbles. Another fact you should know is, it is impossible to fix a leaking rubber hose by over tightening a metal fitting, no matter how much it over tightened, it will never stop. Did you know that regulator threads can be destroyed by over tightening the threads, which will turn your regulator into a paper weight. You would be amazed by how much information torque can tell a person.

In a nutshell, proper torque = proper care.

To elaborate, torque is arguably the easiest part of regulator repair. When somebody can repeatedly do the easiest part of their job correctly it says they probably can do the hardest part of their job also. However, when they routinely mess up the easiest part of their job, they are incapable of performing more complex tasks of regulator service.

Torque does have measureable value, a highly accurate torque wrench will give you a torque value down to the "inch pound." For most applications an ordinary wrench works very well and torque has a sliding scale. Holding the regulator firmly in one hand with the flats of the wrench on the metal fitting, it should not unscrew using only three fingers, that is not enough torque and stinky bologna. Severe over-torque is a full hand on the wrench and you're grunting trying to get it loose, your knuckles are turning white, or you have all your weight bearing down on the wrench, once again that is stinky bologna. Acceptable torque can be measured with a dial torque wrench and by feel. Most regulators I service state a torque valve of 40 inch-pounds to secure the hose to the first stage. With a wrench this means it should be secured firmly but don't be a weakling and don't be Hercules, think of a pickle jar, not to loose, not to tight.

   The other problem happens when somebody decides to play with their regulator. They take their hoses off and they think it is built using tapered pipe threads, so they contaminate their regulator with masses of pipe sealing compound and pipe tape. These compounds first off do not belong on scuba regulator threads. Secondly they can become dislodged and damage the regulator. Use an o-ring seal the way it was designed to operate, without contaminating the regulator and without excessive force.

The next category of problems are related to corrosion and not rinsing the regulator properly. Normally I am able to disassemble a regulator with a bit of finesse. Sometimes it takes a little force and other times it takes more extreme measures. When a regulator is corroded, it will not come apart unless you get creative. First I have to use two tools to distribute the force and avoid cracking the threads, one in the HP port and the other in a low pressure port. When that does not work, I take it to the next level, which is piping hot water in an attempt to expand the metal and break the corrosion. When the piping hot water fails, I take it to the next extreme, which is cold and I throw it in the freezer and wait until it becomes an ice cube. Immediately after it becomes an ice cube, it is thrown back into the piping hot water, from the piping hot water, back into the vise with the two tools to distribute the force between the threads in a second attempt to break it loose.

If all of this fails to work, I am resorted to bringing out a breaker bar. At this point there is some serious corrosion damage present, and if this doesn't get the regulator apart, it is either going to become a paper weight or it's getting shipped back to the factory, as the factory always gets the worst of the worst regulators to work on from repair centers. Either way it will become a very expensive proposition.

Sand is the enemy of all Scuba divers' equipment worldwide and it is a constant problem, as there is constantly more and more of it. I have literally poured beach sand an 1/8 high out of a filter, I've opened alternates which are packed 1/3 full with a cake of sand. Sand can scratch soft materials such as brass, which seals on the low pressure seat of your second stage regulator. Take care of your regulator, don't drag it through the muck mud or sand, get rid of those dangles and secure it to yourself. Your wallet will thank you later when you spend $3.00 for a retainer instead of replacing your old regulator that got dragged across the bottom, broke off coral, filled with sand and dragged through fish poop.

The next batch of problems is unfortunately a very difficult problem to treat. That problem is called "good enough" and, or "making things up as you go along". The Solution to this problem is more manuals than you can shake a stick at, following those manuals and having a good relationship with the manufacture. From Aqualung every regulator has a complete service manual with a standard operating procedure, do's, don'ts and a comprehensive troubleshooting guide. When a problem arises not in the manual, it is a very easy task for me to call them up and get an approved fix.

The inverse of having a good relationship with the manufacture and a stockpile of manuals is like trying to fit a square peg into a round hole, it does not work. I have seen parts, which should have been treated with a high quality lubricant, instead they were treated with a chemical locking compound.

One day I received a first stage regulator, which took me another 15 minutes to take apart, I noticed a broken balance chamber and could not find the broken chip in the regulator, which meant it had been broken for awhile. I ordered a new balance chamber and when it arrived I was in for a shock that it did not fit and I would need a hammer to break it again and make it fit. So I called up Aqualung and as it turns out he knew exactly what the problem was. The regulator was dropped and instead of a round body it was smashed into an oval.

I could go on and on but the bottom line is this. Make sure your service center uses factory kits to rebuild your regulator, accept no substitutions. A good sign of factory parts is packaging. Many factory kits come with an index card sized insert with the company name and regulator model printed on it. Others come with very bold labels of the company and regulator model. However, if you see a bag that looks generic that looks like it came from a hardware store, that is a good indication that you are getting cheap parts, and corners are getting cut. When a good regulator goes bad, chances are good that the next event will be named "When regulators strike back."

End

Made in the USA
Monee, IL
01 March 2021